THE INVENTRESS'S GUIDE TO INVENTING THE RIGHT WAY!

ALL OR NOTHING NOW OR NEVER!

I0527924

WRITTEN BY:
Lisa Ascolese
The Inventress

For Eddie, Brittany, Giana, Olivia Ivy and Iyla
Live each day filled with gratitude and kindness,
laugh and dance everyday like
there's no tomorrow.

Table of Contents

ALL OR NOTHING NOW OR NEVER!

THE INVENTRESS'S GUIDE TO INVENTING THE RIGHT WAY!

ALL OR NOTHING NOW OR NEVER!

Lisa Ascolese
The Inventress

Acknowledgment

First and foremost, I thank God for all things seen and unseen. I extend my deepest gratitude to my family, the constant catalyst behind my strength to navigate challenges that often seemed insurmountable. My parents, my mom, Pauline Williams, the kindest and most nurturing person who ever lived, and my father, Bill Williams, who walked with pure class and confidence, along with my grandmother, Viola J. Miller, who imparted great words of wisdom to me, along with my uncle Alvin, though no longer with us on this side, continue to guide me through their words of wisdom, kindness, encouragement, and faith, which have shaped the person I am today.

A special acknowledgment goes to my pillars of strength: my children, Eddie, Brittany, and Giana, who have been my loudest cheerleaders in life. Their humor, intelligence, love, and kindness are beyond words. Additionally, my granddaughters, Olivia, Ivy, and Iyla, bring immense joy to my daily life, as do my puppies, Winnie and Quimbly. My heartfelt thanks to my sister, Andrea, for being my mentor and inspiration, for always listening all hours of the day and night, for being my kind confidant and faithful friend, and to my brother, Derek, for his positivity and for always lifting me up! All of his children and grandchildren, whose kindness and drive inspire me.

My gratitude goes to my nieces and nephews, Elijah, Zion, Isaiah, Stephanye, Michael, Jordan, JJ, Ricky, Dicotta, Noel, Lennox, Daniel, Donique, and Bryson, as their sense of humor and laughter bring endless joy into my life.

ALL OR NOTHING NOW OR NEVER!

I want to express my gratitude to my wonderful cousin and friend, Jeanette, who I have laughed with for over fifty years; and my dear friend, Marianne, who witnessed my baby girl Giana's birth.

Special thanks to my team, including Tara Ackaway from Social Wise Communications for exceptional support and Michael Duhaylungsod for helping finalize this long-awaited book. Heartfelt thanks to some of my amazing clients and supporters who trust and believe in me. Thank you Cindy Russo for helping me walk through those giant doors at QVC over 25 years ago. I can't name them all; their names would take up the entire book; however, I will acknowledge a few, without whom there would be no story. Kevin and Laurie Lane, Tamara and Sean Turman, Marci Hopkins, Lonnie Montgomery and Kevin Garcia, Sonia Alyene, Yvonne Coston, Lisa Pietracatella, Tutaya Murchison, Cynthia Green, Antonia Tomao. A special acknowledgment goes to Craig McGill, my producer, for helping launch Inventors Spotlight TV. My dedicated (AOWIE) members for always supporting The Association of Women Inventors and Entrepreneurs, are Kimberly A. Ferguson, Linda Vera, Jackie Berman, Danielle Wooley, Edith Anne, Shelley Barnes, Sheryl Hatwood, Elizabeth and Richard Gearhart, Mona Stephen, Maria Lee-Driver, and the list goes on.

My gratitude extends to the various publications I have had the incredible fortune to be in, including Times Square Billboard; thank you, Yvonne Forbes! Black Enterprise Magazine, thank you, Chandra McQueen; Essence Magazine; Ebony Magazine; Forbes Magazine Tara Ackaway, thank you, in addition to countless television shows I have been blessed to appear on, from QVC, HSN, Bravo TV, Own Network and ABC7 "Here and Now"—I must thank the host of "Here and Now," Sandra Bookman, for her kind words and support, and for having me on her show time and time again. Thank you, Tracey Washington Bagley, executive producer of "Here and Now,"

ALL OR NOTHING NOW OR NEVER!

and Delores Spruel, executive producer of "The Kelly and Mark Show." A giant thanks to my celebrity clients—past and present—for your support.

A special thanks and gratitude to Dionne Warwick, who has been especially supportive and kind to me beyond measure for more than twenty years. Jasmine Guy, Alyson Williams, Tyrese Gibson, Carla Hall, Sheryl Lee Ralph, Gloria Gainer, Steve Harvey, Anna Maria Horseford, Nicole Arie Parker, and others, thanks for believing in me and providing invaluable opportunities to work with you all. A sincere thank you to my photographer, Danny Sanchez, for capturing the moment.

ALL OR NOTHING NOW OR NEVER!

"Taking two steps back gives you a clear vision of what's in front of you"

Lisa Marie Ascolese

"When you rise to the top, extend your hand down and lift others higher"

Lisa Marie Ascolese

ALL OR NOTHING NOW OR NEVER!

BIO

Lisa Ascolese, also known as "The Inventress," is a dynamic entrepreneur and inventor with a passion for turning creative ideas into successful products. She was born in London and raised in Brooklyn, New York, by her loving West Indian parents. Lisa is the youngest of three children. Lisa has three wonderful children and three adorable grandchildren. Lisa's early years were marked by a vibrant and imaginative mind. At the age of nine, she began modifying items around her childhood home, foreshadowing the innovative path she would later embark on.

As an adult, Lisa founded her own product development company, "Inventing A to Z" (inventingatoz.com), where she guides inventors through the process of bringing their ideas from concept to fruition in the most effective way possible. Over the past twenty-five years, she has designed, manufactured, and sold hundreds of inventions, showcasing her products on major platforms such as QVC, HSN, ShopHQ, and in retail stores.

In addition to her role as a successful entrepreneur, Lisa is the founder of "Inventors Spotlight TV" (inventorsspotlighttv.com), her own television musically inspired shopping network, providing a platform for inventors to showcase their creations. Recognizing the importance of mentorship and support in the entrepreneurial journey, Lisa launched the non-profit organization "The Association of Women Inventors & Entrepreneurs Conference" (AOWIE). This is a musically inspired conference that was created (www.aowie.com) to empower and connect aspiring inventors and entrepreneurs. Lisa also has a podcast called "The Inventress Podcast," where she invites inventors and entrepreneurs to share their fascinating stories and their journeys.

ALL OR NOTHING NOW OR NEVER!

"The Inventress" has gained recognition not only for her business acumen but also for her appearances on Bravo TV, ABC7, Own Television, Sirius XM Radio, IHeart Radio, and in many major publications such as Black Enterprise Magazine, Ebony Magazine, Forbes Magazine, Essence Magazine, and countless others. Lisa's diverse range of her own inventions includes The Bosom Buddy Nursing Cape, Bun-Tie hair accessory, Wrap and Store Organizer, Perfect Pockets Organizer, Lugeze Bows, Hanger Tights, The Wobble Stopper, and the list goes on.

As an inventor, mentor, and entrepreneur, Lisa's goal is to see all inventors succeed. Her mission is to uplift others, advocating for mutual support with her motto, "Lifting Each Other Up Two Hands At A Time, And Sometimes You Need A Foot." Lisa is also committed to "bridging the gap between ambition and success," embodying her second mission statement, dedication to empowering others. Lisa Ascolese continues to make a lasting impact in the world of invention and entrepreneurship.

I never imagined I would be where I am today, but here I am. As a child, creativity flowed through me, and when asked about my aspirations, I always dreamed of being a mom first, an airline stewardess, and a model. My dreams evolved as I grew older, considering careers such as law, computer science, singer-songwriter, nurse, doctor, or dentist at various stages. Although I didn't pursue all those paths, life led me to college for computer science. I modeled for a short period, became a mommy, wrote songs, and published books, which was an unexpected path, for sure! Transforming words into lullaby books, all for my children and now, grandchildren.

ALL OR NOTHING NOW OR NEVER!

Inventing products, patenting, trademarking, and copywriting all became unexpected blessings in my life. Most importantly, watching my three children grow to be the most incredible people on the planet.

My journey embraced unexpected turns, from working as a dental assistant to building up and selling two cleaning services, creating a successful catering service, and designing food platters. I also cared for someone without family, integrating him into our home until the final days of his life. As life unfolded, fulfilling aspects of my nursing aspirations came to fruition. Through faith and perseverance, I've invented, manufactured, and sold hundreds of products, realizing the power of belief in making the seemingly impossible possible.

The moral of my story echoes: what you believe and work toward can manifest in your life. Nothing was handed to me on a silver platter; every achievement was earned through hard work, dedication, and the grace of God. As I continue this journey, I embrace growth and improvement, always believing that success is achievable when you have faith. Here's my favorite verse from the book of Matthew 7.7, "Ask and it will be given to you; seek, and you will find; knock, and the door will be open to you."

ALL OR NOTHING NOW OR NEVER!

ONE

THE POWER OF NAMING IT AND CLAIMING IT

Embarking on the transformative journey of bringing your invention to life, the initial step is not just pivotal but also exhilarating: the art of Naming and Claiming. This chapter delves into the intricacies of crafting an identity for your creation that goes beyond mere nomenclature—it's about sculpting a brand that resonates profoundly with your intended audience.

Choosing Your Product's Name: The Alchemy of Essence:
- Begin by immersing yourself in the very core of your invention, unraveling its essence, purpose, and unique selling points.
- Engage in a spirited brainstorming session, encouraging creativity and exploration of various name options that vividly encapsulate the uniqueness and spirit of your creation. I must add that when you are brainstorming, always do it in the company of positive people who have your best interests in mind and those who are openly creative.
- Prioritize attributes such as memorability, ease of pronunciation, and alignment with your overarching brand vision to ensure a lasting and impactful impression. When mentally conceiving your product, invest your love in it, akin to the care given to a newborn. I'm not equating a child to a product, but the analogy serves to underscore the significance of giving your creation a name—it becomes real.

Choosing a product name should capture consumer attention and convey its purpose. Some inventors opt for complex acronyms, often tied to family names, making marketing more challenging.

For instance, "fdmrncarg" may represent a toy car using family initials, but the complexity makes it challenging for the brain to grasp and remember.

Contrast, simple, and descriptive names like some of my products have simple and easily recognizable names, such as "The Bosom Buddy breastfeeding cape" or my "Wrap and Store Organizer" as seen on QVC, my perfect Pockets Organizer, as seen on QVC, and HSN, my Bun-tie hair accessory, as seen on QVC, effectively communicate the product's function, making marketing more straightforward. These names not only roll off the tongue but also tell a story about the product.

On the contrary, names like "pdmrtyupin," where the name is embedded within the letters, pose challenges for memorization. This pin, designed collaboratively by a family, may have sentimental value, but its intricate name doesn't easily stick in the mind.

In upcoming sections, I'll delve into my journey with QVC, sharing how I entered and sustained a presence on this renowned platform for over twenty-five years and counting. Keep reading for insights into this exciting chapter of my career!

Claiming Your Product: Safeguarding Your Brainchild:
- Navigate the labyrinth of legalities by proactively securing your product's name through the formal process of trademark registration. This not only protects your creation but also establishes your exclusive rights to its identity.
- Grasp the profound significance of intellectual property protection, understanding how it fortifies the foundation of your invention against potential challenges and limitations.

Domain Name: The Virtual Threshold:
- Strategically choose a domain name that seamlessly mirrors your product's identity, aligning with the essence you've uncovered, and ensure its availability for registration.
- Recognize the paramount importance of early domain acquisition, as it lays the groundwork for your imminent online presence, serving as the virtual threshold for your audience to explore and engage with your invention.

Building Your Website: The Digital Facade:
- Astutely allocate business funds not only to procure your chosen domain but also to initiate the meticulous development of your website.
- Understand that a professionally crafted online presence is not merely a facade; it is a dynamic and powerful tool for introducing your invention to a global audience. Explore elements like user-friendly design, compelling content, and seamless navigation to enhance your digital impact.

Business Structure: The Fortress of Flexibility:
- Opt for the protective shield of an LLC (limited liability company) to enjoy both legal security and operational flexibility. This business structure shields your personal assets while allowing adaptability to the evolving needs of your enterprise.
- Familiarize yourself with the advantageous separation of personal and business assets, recognizing it as an elemental aspect of responsible entrepreneurship that contributes to long-term stability.

Opening a Business Checking Account: Financial Clarity and Efficiency:

- Establish a dedicated business checking account beneath the protective umbrella of your LLC, promoting financial clarity and streamlining the management of your growing enterprise.
- Recognize the pivotal role this step plays in maintaining financial efficiency, tracking expenses, and ensuring a clear demarcation between personal and business finances.

As you traverse the enthralling landscape of naming, claiming, and laying the cornerstone of your business foundation, remember that each stride is a fundamental building block for your forthcoming triumph. The potency of a meticulously chosen name, legally fortified rights, and a robust online presence will serve as the compass guiding your invention toward prominence in the market. Anticipate the revelations of Chapter Two, where we plunge into the intricacies of product development, propelling your concept to the next echelon of realization. We will discuss the importance of brand recognition. Below are key examples of brands you recognize in the blink of an eye:

Amazon	Apple
Macdonalds	Dell
Microsoft	Tesla
Lugeze bows	BMW
Inventing A to Z	Facebook
Coca-Cola	Netflix
Mr. Clean	BET
Shark Tank	OWN
Google	

Three seconds *tops!*

When you fall down,

you've got to get up,

staying down

is not an option.

Lisa Marie Ascolese

TWO

BRINGING YOUR VISION TO REALITY - THE ART OF PRODUCT DEVELOPMENT

With the foundational elements of your invention established, Chapter Two delves into the captivating world of product development. This phase marks the transition from conceptualization to the tangible realization of your creation, requiring a strategic approach to ensure your product not only meets but also exceeds expectations.

Concept Refinement: Sketching the Blueprint:
- Begin by revisiting the essence of your initial concept, taking into account feedback from potential users and insights gained through market research. How do you do this? The World Wide Web. See who your competitors are, and steer clear of copying what is on the market. Let me be clear: there is always room for improvement with any product on the market, so don't get discouraged if you see a product that has similarities. Look carefully at ways you can improve upon your product idea based on your research and move in that direction. Although great minds think alike, all of your ideas are unique.
- Embark on the creative journey of creating a detailed blueprint or sketch that not only captures the aesthetic aspects but also outlines the functionality and user experience. This blueprint will serve as a guiding map throughout the development process.

Prototyping: From Paper to Prototype:

- Enter the prototyping phase, where your concept transforms from two-dimensional sketches to a three-dimensional prototype. This tangible model is instrumental in assessing functionality, identifying potential improvements, and gaining a realistic visualization of your invention.
- Collaborate with experienced designers and engineers who can bring your vision to life, ensuring that the prototype aligns seamlessly with your original concept.

Material Selection: Building Blocks of Quality:

- Carefully consider the materials that will compose your product, keeping in mind factors such as purpose, durability, and aesthetics.
- Assess the environmental impact of your material choices, along with production costs and overall sustainability. Striking the right balance is essential for the success of your product.

Testing and Iteration: Perfecting the Prototype:

- Initiate comprehensive testing of your prototype, scrutinizing every aspect to identify potential flaws, weaknesses, or areas for improvement.
- Embrace an iterative mindset, allowing the insights gained from testing to guide subsequent refinements. Continuous improvement is key to ensuring your product meets high-quality standards.

Regulatory Compliance: Navigating the Standards:

- Navigate the intricate landscape of industry regulations and standards relevant to your product.
- Ensure that your invention adheres to safety, quality, and any other pertinent guidelines, guaranteeing both consumer trust and market compliance.

Create a Drawing of Your Product: Visualizing the Vision:

- Collaborate with skilled illustrators or leverage design software to create a detailed drawing or rendering of your product. This visual representation is a powerful tool for effectively communicating the uniqueness and value of your invention to potential investors, manufacturers, and consumers.
- The drawing serves as a compelling preview, allowing stakeholders to grasp the aesthetic appeal and features of your creation.

In navigating the complexities of product development, creativity and adaptability remain your allies. As you refine your concept into a tangible prototype, remember that each phase contributes to the masterpiece in progress. Chapter Three will guide you through the pivotal stages of sourcing manufacturers, preparing for production, and strategically positioning your invention for market success. Your product is evolving—let's continue sculpting it into a remarkable reality.

Your words
are the most
powerful reflection
of who *you are*
or who *you can*
become

Lisa Marie Ascolese

THREE

CRAFTING EXCELLENCE - PROTOTYPING AND PROTECTING YOUR VISION

As your invention takes shape in the development phase, Chapter Three delves into the intricacies of detailing your product to create a prototype. This crucial stage not only refines your concept also lays the groundwork for a tangible representation of your vision. Additionally, it emphasizes the importance of safeguarding your intellectual property with a non-disclosure agreement (NDA) when sharing information with potential collaborators.

Detailed Product Specifications: The Blueprint of Precision:
- Articulate and document comprehensive product specifications that meticulously outline every aspect of your invention.
- Include details on dimensions, materials, color schemes, functionality, and any unique features that define your product. Precision in specification is paramount in translating your vision into a tangible prototype.

Technical Drawings and CAD Models: Engineering Precision:
- Collaborate with skilled engineers and designers to create technical drawings and computer-aided design (CAD) models based on your detailed specifications.
- These drawings serve as the technical blueprint, providing precise measurements and specifications that guide the manufacturing process. These CAD models offer a three-dimensional digital representation for a more comprehensive understanding.

Prototyping Technologies: From Virtual to Reality:
- Explore various prototyping technologies that align with your product's complexity and materials.
- From 3D printing to CNC machining, choose the method that best captures the essence of your invention. Prototyping allows you to physically test and refine your concept, bridging the gap between the virtual and the tangible.

Choosing the Right Prototype Materials: A Symphony of Quality:
- Consider the ideal materials for your prototype, ensuring they align with the final product's intended characteristics.
- Evaluate the feasibility of using materials that closely mimic those intended for mass production, providing a more accurate representation of your invention.

Non-Disclosure Agreement (NDA): Protecting Your Intellectual Property:
- Prioritize the protection of your intellectual property by having a well-drafted non-disclosure agreement (NDA) ready.
- Ensure that anyone involved in the prototyping process, from collaborators to manufacturers, signs the NDA before gaining access to sensitive information. This legal document safeguards your innovative ideas and proprietary information.

Iterative Prototyping: Refining the Fine Details:
- Embrace an iterative approach to prototyping, recognizing that the first prototype may reveal areas for improvement.
- Work closely with your development team to refine the prototype based on testing results and user feedback. This iterative process ensures that your final product meets the highest standards of quality and functionality.

User Testing and Feedback: Validating Your Concept:
- Conduct thorough user testing to gather valuable insights into the practicality and user experience of your prototype.
- Solicit feedback from a diverse group of potential users to identify any potential improvements or adjustments needed before moving to mass production. Please note: when you are creating a prototype, you are creating a proof of concept for the manufacturer, meaning that if the look and maneuverability are not perfect but they illustrate the function, the manufacturer will be able to advance the functionality and appearance of the product; hence, having clear instructions and details about how the product should look and operate is paramount.

Documentation for Manufacturing: A Seamless Transition:
- Create comprehensive documentation that details every aspect of the prototype, including materials, dimensions, and manufacturing processes.

- This documentation serves as a seamless transition guide for manufacturers, ensuring they can faithfully replicate your vision in the final production phase.

By meticulously detailing your product and protecting your intellectual property with a robust NDA, you not only guide the prototyping process but also secure your innovative concepts. As you progress toward Chapter Four, which delves into sourcing manufacturers and preparing for production, you are well-equipped to turn your prototype into a market-ready reality. Your invention is reaching new heights—let's continue crafting excellence.

Reach *your* goals *and* dreams *on your own* timelines, *but give* yourself *a* timeline.

Lisa Marie Ascolese

FOUR

BUILDING A PROTOTYPE FOR PROOF OF CONCEPT - A METHODICAL APPROACH

In Chapter Four, we embark on the pivotal journey of building a prototype, a tangible representation that validates the proof of concept for your invention. These five simple steps guide you through the process, ensuring a methodical and effective approach.

Refining Technical Drawings: Precision in Planning:
- Begin by revisiting and refining the technical drawings and CAD models created in the previous chapter.
- Collaborate closely with engineers and designers to ensure that every detail is meticulously represented, creating a blueprint that serves as the foundation for your prototype. It is important to work with people you trust. Just because a company tells you they can make a product fast does not make them a good company. Through my experiences, inventing my own products as well as products for my clients has always been a mystery to me. I say this because, just when you think a product should be easy and fast to develop, that's not always the case; it's a surprise. Sometimes, the products you assume will be created quickly are small and can be the most challenging. My most successful products in terms of turnaround times have been fabric-based, but let me be clear: never without flaws. FYI, there is always more than one prototype; prepare for many!

Selecting Prototype Materials: Translating Vision into Reality:

- Based on the refined technical drawings, carefully choose materials for the prototype that mirror the intended characteristics of the final product.
- Consider the feasibility of using materials that closely resemble those planned for mass production. This selection is crucial to achieving an accurate representation of your invention during the proof-of-concept stage.

Prototype Fabrication: Bridging the Virtual and Tangible:

- Utilize advanced prototyping technologies such as 3D printing, CNC machining, or other appropriate methods based on the complexity of your invention.
- Collaborate with skilled prototypers to bring your virtual designs into the tangible realm. This phase is where the concept takes physical form, allowing you to assess its functionality and make necessary adjustments.

Functional Testing: Ensuring Viability:

- Conduct rigorous functional testing to evaluate how well the prototype aligns with your initial concept.
- Identify any potential issues or areas for improvement through hands-on testing and simulations. This step is crucial for ensuring that your invention not only meets but also exceeds performance expectations.

User Feedback: Validating User Experience:

- Solicit feedback from a diverse group of users who represent your target audience.
- Gauge their experiences, preferences, and any challenges encountered during interactions with the prototype. This valuable input provides insights into user expectations and helps refine the design for enhanced usability.

Throughout these steps, maintaining an iterative mindset is key. Each round of refinement and testing brings you closer to a prototype that authentically represents your vision and demonstrates the viability of your invention.

Practical Considerations:
- Budget Allocation: Be mindful of budget constraints during the prototype-building phase. Prioritize essential features and functionalities to ensure cost-effective development.
- Collaborative Communication: Foster open communication with your development team and prototype manufacturers. Regular updates, feedback sessions, and collaborative problem-solving contribute to a smoother prototyping process.
- Documentation: Document every step of the prototype-building process comprehensively. This documentation will not only guide further development but also serve as a valuable resource for potential manufacturers.

Building a prototype as proof of concept is a crucial stage in bringing your invention to life. As we move forward to Chapter Five, which explores the intricacies of sourcing manufacturers and preparing for production, your meticulously crafted prototype sets the stage for a successful transition from concept to reality. Your invention is gaining momentum; let's continue this exciting journey.

In the intricate process of designing prototypes, I frequently turn to my local dry-cleaning establishment for a valuable resource—skilled seamstresses. Seeking assistance in sewing products and creating patterns, especially for fabric-based items, has proven to be an ingenious and cost-effective solution.

This collaborative approach not only streamlines the prototype development process but also holds the potential to save considerable time and money. By harnessing the expertise available within the local community, I not only enhance the precision of the prototype but also contribute to an efficient transition when selecting the manufacturer for the final product. This practice reflects a resourceful and community-oriented mindset, emphasizing the idea that innovation often thrives in unexpected and local spaces.

PERFECT POCKETS

DESIGNED BY:
Lisa Ascolese
The Inventress

Before

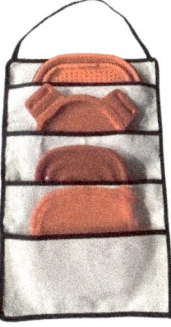

After

Live
in the greatness
and glory God
created for
you today

Lisa Marie Ascolese

FIVE

FORTIFYING YOUR CREATIONS
- PROTECTING INTELLECTUAL PROPERTIES, INVENTION, BRAND, AND LOGO

As you navigate the intricate landscape of turning your invention into a market-ready reality, Chapter Five serves as a pivotal guide to protect the core assets of your enterprise: your intellectual properties, including your invention, brand, and logo. This comprehensive exploration aims to secure the fruits of your creativity and innovation.

Intellectual Property Assessment: Defining the Scope:

- Undertake a comprehensive assessment of your intellectual properties, encompassing your invention, brand, and logo.
- Conduct a diligent patent search to ascertain the uniqueness of your invention and identify potential conflicts. Simultaneously, explore trademark registration for your brand name and logo to establish legal ownership and prevent unauthorized usage.

Patenting Your Invention: Shielding Innovation with Legal Armor:

- Collaborate with a seasoned patent attorney to navigate the intricacies of the patent application process.
- Choose the most appropriate type of patent—whether utility, design, or plant patents—based on the nature of your invention. A granted patent provides exclusive rights, preventing others from making, using, or selling your invention without your permission.

Trademarking Your Brand and Logo: Identity Protection Strategies:

- Engage a trademark attorney to guide you through the intricacies of registering your brand name and logo.
- The process involves conducting a thorough search to ensure uniqueness, followed by the submission of trademark applications. Trademarks provide legal protection, safeguarding your brand identity and preventing unauthorized usage.

Documentation and Record-Keeping: A Pillar of Legal Defense:

- Establish a robust system for documenting the entire development process of your invention.
- Maintain detailed records, including concept sketches, technical drawings, and prototyping details. Keep meticulous records of trademark and patent applications, correspondence with attorneys, and any communication related to intellectual property. This documentation serves as a crucial defense in potential legal disputes.

Non-Disclosure Agreements (NDAs): Safeguarding Collaborations:

- Continue to leverage non-disclosure agreements (NDAs) when entering collaborations with external entities, such as manufacturers, investors, or potential partners. Craft NDAs that clearly outline the confidential nature of your invention, brand, and logo details. This not only fosters collaboration but also provides legal recourse in case of any breaches of confidentiality.

Regular Intellectual Property Audits: Proactive Vigilance:
- Schedule periodic intellectual property audits to reevaluate and update your protection strategies.
- Stay abreast of any changes in intellectual property laws and regulations. Regular audits ensure that your protection mechanisms remain robust and effective in the dynamic landscape of innovation and business.

Enforcing Your Rights: Vigilant Protection in Action:
- Be prepared to take legal action to enforce your intellectual property rights if an infringement occurs.
- Vigilantly monitor the market for any unauthorized use of your invention, brand, or logo. Swift and decisive legal action is crucial to maintaining the integrity of your creations and brand identity.

International Protection Considerations: Expanding Safeguards Globally:
- Explore international patent and trademark protections if your business operations expand globally.
- Understand the nuances of intellectual property laws in different countries and take proactive steps to secure your rights internationally. International protections provide a crucial defense against potential infringements on a global scale.

As you diligently implement these strategies to protect your intellectual properties, you create a solid foundation for the success and longevity of your business.

Moving forward to Chapter Six, we will explore the strategic positioning of your invention in the market and effective marketing strategies to ensure its successful introduction to the world. Your intellectual properties are now under a shield—let's continue this journey toward triumph.

It's important for me to lift some of this very heavy material I have laid on your shoulders. My suggestion is to use a patent attorney you can trust to guide you through the process. They will do the heavy lifting for you.

Walk

in faith *and*

fortify it

with more faith

Lisa Marie Ascolese

SIX

STRATEGIC MARKET ANALYSIS - PAVING THE PATH TO INFORMED MANUFACTURING

Before venturing into full-scale manufacturing, Chapter Six serves as the compass that guides you through the critical phase of understanding your market. This chapter delves into the nuanced process of market analysis, emphasizing the importance of knowing your competitors. This strategic understanding ensures that your manufacturing efforts align with the needs, preferences, and dynamics of your target audience. We touched on this in the previous chapter; however, I just need to reiterate how important it is to stay positive when you see a product on the market that has similar features and characteristics to yours. There are hundreds of cell phones on the market, as well as coffee pots and a whole host of other products that are replications of what exists. Keep an open mind and create with the uniqueness God gave you.

Market Research Essentials: Gaining Insightful Perspectives:
- Initiate comprehensive market research to gain deep insights into your industry, target audience, and potential market trends.
- Utilize a mix of primary and secondary research methods, including surveys, interviews, competitor analysis, and industry reports. This foundation of knowledge is pivotal to shaping your manufacturing strategy.

Identifying Target Demographics: Precision in Audience Understanding:

- Define and profile your target demographics with meticulous detail. Understand the characteristics, preferences, and behaviors of your potential customers. This knowledge allows you to tailor your product features and marketing strategies to resonate with your intended audience.

Market Trends and Dynamics: Staying Ahead of the Curve:

- Stay abreast of current market trends and dynamics that may impact your product or industry. You can do this by researching social media, as well as taking a deep dive into Google searches.
- Identify emerging trends, consumer preferences, and technological advancements. This foresight allows you to position your product as innovative and aligned with market expectations.

SWOT Analysis: Evaluating Strengths, Weaknesses, Opportunities, and Threats:

- Conduct a thorough SWOT analysis of your business and product concept.
- Identify the internal strengths and weaknesses of your venture, as well as external opportunities and threats in the market. This analysis provides a holistic view, guiding your manufacturing decisions with a strategic edge.

Competitor Analysis: Learning from the Landscape:

- Examine and analyze your competitors within the market.
- Identify their strengths, weaknesses, unique selling points, and market positioning. This knowledge is instrumental in differentiating your product and developing a competitive edge.

Unique Selling Proposition (USP): Carving Your Niche:

- Define a clear unique selling proposition (USP) that sets your product apart in the market.
- Highlight what makes your invention distinct and superior to competitors. Your USP becomes a central element in your marketing strategy and product differentiation.

Market Segmentation: Tailoring for Diverse Audiences:

- Divide your target market into segments based on specific characteristics, needs, and preferences.
- Tailor your product features, marketing messages, and distribution channels to cater to the unique demands of each segment. This personalized approach enhances the relevance of your product.

Price Sensitivity and Positioning: Strategic Pricing Strategies:

- Understand the price sensitivity of your target audience and position your product accordingly.
- Determine whether your product will be positioned as a premium offering, a mid-range option, or a budget-friendly solution. Strategic pricing enhances your competitiveness in the market.

Regulatory Compliance: Navigating Legal Landscape:
- Familiarize yourself with industry regulations and standards applicable to your product.
- Ensure that your manufacturing plans align with legal requirements and quality standards. Regulatory compliance is essential for building trust with both consumers and retailers.

Feedback and Iteration: Refining Based on Market Response:
- Gather feedback from potential customers, industry experts, and focus groups.
- Use this feedback to iterate on your product concept, features, and marketing strategy. This iterative process ensures that your manufacturing plans align closely with market expectations.

By immersing yourself in a thorough understanding of your market, you lay a foundation for manufacturing that is not only efficient but also aligned with market demand. As we transition to Chapter Seven, which explores the critical aspects of sourcing a reliable manufacturer, you are equipped with strategic insights to navigate the manufacturing landscape successfully. Your journey toward bringing your invention to life is gaining clarity—let's continue with purpose and precision.

How can we find a perfect manufacturer for our products?
- Navigating Options: Explore diverse manufacturing options, from local to international, considering factors such as cost, quality, and production capacity.

- Supplier Networks: Tap into industry networks, attend trade shows, and engage with online platforms to connect with reputable manufacturers.
- Quality Assurance: Prioritize manufacturers with a proven track record of quality assurance and adherence to production standards. Transparent Communication: Establish open and transparent communication with potential manufacturers, clearly articulating your product specifications and expectations.
- Visit Facilities: Whenever possible, conduct site visits to manufacturing facilities to assess their capabilities, quality control measures, and overall operations.
- References and Reviews: Seek references and read reviews from other businesses that have collaborated with the manufacturer, gaining insights into their reliability and performance.
- Negotiation and Contracts: Skillfully negotiate terms and conditions, ensuring clarity in contracts regarding production timelines, quality standards, and pricing structures.

Be the attraction of greatness, goodness and kindness and that's what you will attract

Lisa Marie Ascolese

CRAFTING SUCCESS - SOURCING A RELIABLE MANUFACTURER WITH STRATEGIC PRECISION. ALWAYS BE RESPECTFUL AND KIND

As you transition from intellectual property protection to the tangible realm of production, Chapter Seven becomes the cornerstone of bringing your invention to market. This chapter intricately guides you through the process of sourcing a reliable manufacturer, emphasizing the importance of strategic decision-making to avoid overproduction and maximize market viability.

Understanding Your Production Needs: A Blueprint for Manufacturing:
- Begin by clearly defining your production requirements. Understand the volume, specifications, and quality standards necessary for manufacturing your invention.
- Collaborate with your development team and consult industry experts to ascertain the optimal production scale and capabilities needed to meet market demand.

Researching and Identifying Potential Manufacturers: The Quest for Reliability:
- Conduct extensive research to identify potential manufacturers who specialize in producing items similar to your invention.

- Scrutinize their track record, reputation, and production capabilities. Seek referrals and testimonials to ensure you partner with a reliable manufacturer committed to delivering quality results.

Communication and Collaboration: Building Strong Partnerships:
- Establish open lines of communication with potential manufacturers. Clearly convey your expectations, quality standards, and production timelines.
- Foster collaborative relationships by addressing any concerns or questions they may have. Effective communication lays the foundation for a successful and enduring partnership.

Sample Production: Assessing Quality and Compatibility:
- Initiate a small-scale sample production to assess the manufacturer's capabilities and the quality of the produced items.
- Use this phase to identify any potential issues and ensure that the manufacturer can meet your specifications. Make the necessary adjustments before proceeding to full-scale production.

Negotiating Terms and Agreements: A Fair and Clear Partnership:
- Engage in transparent negotiations regarding production costs, lead times, and quality control measures.

- Draft comprehensive manufacturing agreements that clearly outline expectations, responsibilities, and any penalties for non-compliance. Clarity in these agreements is essential for building a strong and mutually beneficial partnership.

Securing Buyers Before Full-Scale Production: Mitigating Risks of Overproduction:

- Adopt a strategic approach by securing commitments from buyers before initiating full-scale production.
- Utilize pre-orders, letters of intent, or agreements with distributors to gauge market demand. This approach minimizes the risk of overproducing items that may not have a ready market.

Monitoring Production and Quality Control: Ensuring Excellence Every Step:

- Implement robust systems for monitoring the production process and ensuring adherence to quality standards.
- Regularly communicate with the manufacturer, conduct site visits if possible, and establish quality control measures to maintain consistency and excellence in production.

Shipping and Logistics: Streamlining the Supply Chain:

- Develop a comprehensive shipping and logistics plan to efficiently move products from the manufacturer to your storage or distribution centers.
- Optimize the supply chain to minimize delays and reduce costs associated with transportation and warehousing.

Strategic Inventory Management: Balancing Supply and Demand:

- Implement a strategic inventory management system to balance supply and demand effectively.
- Avoid the pitfalls of overstocking by maintaining an inventory level that aligns with market demand. This approach ensures that you can meet customer needs without the burden of excess unsold merchandise.

Continuous Evaluation and Adaptation: Navigating Market Dynamics:

- Regularly evaluate market trends, customer feedback, and sales data to adapt your production strategy accordingly.
- Stay agile and responsive to changing market dynamics, allowing you to refine your production approach and maintain a competitive edge.

By approaching the intricate landscape of manufacturing with a strategic mindset, you not only ensure the establishment of trustworthy partnerships but also cultivate an environment of kindness and understanding within the production process. This approach not only benefits your venture but also contributes to the well-being of all involved stakeholders.

In navigating this chapter, which serves as a guide to effective marketing strategies, let's underscore the importance of kindness as an integral element of your business philosophy. In a world where transactions often dominate, infusing kindness into your manufacturing endeavors creates a ripple effect of positive energy. It involves respecting the time and efforts of your manufacturing partners, valuing the skills of the workforce, and fostering an environment of collaboration and mutual support.

Kindness in manufacturing extends beyond the product itself; it encompasses the relationships forged and the impact on the broader community. By prioritizing fair labor practices, sustainable sourcing, and ethical manufacturing processes, you contribute to a supply chain that reflects the values of compassion and responsibility.

As we embark on Chapter Eight, let's weave the fabric of your business not only with strategic insights but also with a thread of kindness. In doing so, we not only create successful products but also build a legacy of compassion and empathy within the entrepreneurial realm.

Take pride

in your work

and your work

will work *for you*

Lisa Marie Ascolese

EIGTH

AMPLIFYING PRESENCE - STRATEGIC MARKETING FOR RETAIL SUCCESS

As your invention takes physical form and production gears up, Chapter Eight becomes the linchpin in your journey, guiding you through the intricacies of marketing. This chapter delves into the essentials of positioning your product in retail stores, emphasizing the significance of a barcode for packaging, and leveraging an array of marketing tools, including social media platforms and television shopping networks, to bolster your product's visibility and appeal.

Barcode Implementation: A Key to Retail Accessibility:

- Understand the importance of barcodes in the retail landscape. Barcodes facilitate seamless inventory management and sales transactions.
- Acquire a unique barcode for your product through the official channels, ensuring compliance with industry standards. The barcode becomes an essential component of your packaging, enhancing your product's marketability.

Packaging Design: Merging Aesthetics and Functionality:

- Craft packaging that not only showcases the uniqueness of your invention but also accommodates the barcode seamlessly.
- Consider the visual appeal, durability, and practicality of your packaging. It serves as the first point of contact with potential buyers, making a lasting impression.

Understanding Retail Requirements: Tailoring Your Approach:

- Research and comprehend the specific requirements of retail stores where you aim to showcase your product. How do you do this? You can Google the requirements that each retail store requires. You can also sign up as a vendor, and you will see exactly what each retail store expects from the vendor.
- Adapt your marketing materials, packaging, and presentation to align with the preferences and standards of target retailers. This tailored approach enhances your chances of securing shelf space.

Building Relationships with Retail Buyers: Personalized Engagement:

- Develop a personalized approach when engaging with retail buyers. It is very important to create a subject line that stands out when you are emailing the buyers. When I am sending emails to QVC, HSN, or retail store buyers, I start with a subject line that is guaranteed to grab their attention. For example, if you are presenting a hot new product—the first of its kind, never seen before—that's what you would say!! HOT HOT HOT NEW PRODUCT! Showcase the uniqueness and market potential of your product.
- Establish clear communication channels, providing buyers with comprehensive information and addressing any inquiries promptly. As I prepare my product presentation for QVC, HSN, or any retail store, I plan ahead, assuming what they will ask me for before they ask. In other words, if I am presenting a skincare line, I need to have proof that the formulation works by providing before and after photos and any testing that is required.

If you are working with a scientist or a lab, they should be able to provide you with lab tests and formulation ingredients, as well as test them for safe use on the skin. The reason you do this is to cut down on time and the frustration of unnecessary extra emails. Keep in mind: time is money! Again, have as much information about the product and its visibility together before you present it. You will appear more organized and polished to prospective buyers; dress your product and yourself to impress! Be kind and respectful with your words; you are working with people just like you. Building positive relationships fosters trust and collaboration.

Creating a Compelling Brand Story: Connecting with Consumers:

- Creating a Compelling Brand Story: Connecting with Consumers: Develop a compelling brand narrative that resonates with consumers. Communicate the story behind your invention, emphasizing its value and relevance. What is the reason why the customer should buy your product? Tell your story with passion and authenticity.

- Craft a brand story that not only captivates retail buyers but also creates a connection with end consumers. A strong brand narrative enhances the marketability of your product.

Utilizing Social Media Platforms - A Dynamic Marketing Arsenal:

- Leverage the power of social media platforms to create buzz around your product.

- Develop a comprehensive social media strategy, incorporating platforms such as Instagram, Facebook, Twitter, and others relevant to your target audience. Utilize engaging content, visuals, and storytelling to build anticipation and interest. It's important to use your brand and logo consistently so you start to become a recognizable brand.

Content Marketing: Educational and Informative Outreach:
- Implement a content marketing strategy that educates and informs your target audience.
- Utilize blog posts, articles, videos, and other content formats to highlight the features, benefits, and unique selling points of your invention. Position yourself as an authority in your industry, building credibility and trust.

Influencer Collaborations: Leveraging Trusted Voices:
- Explore collaborations with influencers or thought leaders in your industry.
- Influencers can amplify the reach of your product, reaching a broader audience. Ensure that influencers align with your brand values and can authentically represent your product.

Promotional Campaigns and Events: Creating Buzz:
- Plan and execute promotional campaigns and events to generate excitement around your product.
- Consider launch events, limited-time promotions, or exclusive offers to incentivize purchases and create a sense of urgency.

Monitoring and Analyzing Marketing Performance: Data-Driven Adjustments:

- Implement analytics tools to monitor the performance of your marketing efforts.
- Analyze data on consumer engagement, conversion rates, and sales trends. Use these insights to refine your marketing strategy, optimizing it for maximum impact. Connect with podcasters who promote products. I have a podcast called "The Inventress Podcast." On my platform, we showcase and discuss all of the details about the product, and most importantly, we target the right consumers when we launch the podcast on all social media platforms. Now you are ready and prepared to showcase your product to prospective retail stores or shopping networks. I know all of this might sound overwhelming; take one step at a time, and you will get it done!

By mastering the art of strategic marketing, you position your invention for success in the competitive retail landscape.

As we progress to Chapter Nine, we will explore crucial aspects of customer feedback, post-launch adjustments, and maintaining a thriving presence in the market. Your journey is reaching new heights —let's continue to soar with purpose and precision.

Throughout our shared journey, I'll be imparting numerous positive affirmations. These affirmations aim to reinforce the understanding that success is not only a decision but an attainable reality. To reach that destination, you need the right tools and insights. Here are some of the key ingredients from my personal repertoire that I proudly offer to you: faith, patience, passion, positivity, and the resilience to rise after a fall.

I follow a simple three-second rule: when life knocks you down, you have three seconds to get back up; otherwise, you risk staying down for too long. While this may seem straightforward, I acknowledge the challenges it presents. Surrounding yourself with positive influences —those who uplift and inspire you—is crucial. Moreover, asking for what you need with genuine intent ensures that you receive the support you seek. One of my guiding verses from the Bible is Matthew 7:7 "Ask and you will receive, knock and the door will be open to you, seek and you will find."

Moving forward in your product development and entrepreneurial journey, having a mentor is paramount. A mentor should offer positive and constructive advice, steering away from mere criticism. It's worth noting that many of the world's most successful individuals, such as Oprah Winfrey, Gail King, and Michelle Obama, have benefited from both mentorship and being mentors. It's a reciprocal relationship that propels personal and professional growth.

Answer *your* calling *and* do *what* you *do* best

Lisa Marie Ascolese

THE HEARTBEAT OF SUCCESS - NURTURING PASSION, FAITH, AND UNSHAKEABLE BELIEF IN YOUR PRODUCT

In the tapestry of entrepreneurship, Chapter Nine unfolds as a pivotal chapter, delving into the intrinsic elements that breathe life into your journey: passion, faith, and unyielding belief in your product. This chapter not only emphasizes the crucial role these elements play but also explores practical strategies to foster and harness their transformative power.

Passion: The Unbridled Fuel of Innovation:
- Reconnect with the initial spark that ignited your journey. Passion is the unbridled energy that propels you forward, fuels innovation, and permeates every facet of your venture. There may be people who tell you that you are too passionate about your product; don't listen to the noise from naysayers. Please make sure you do get positive and constructive input about your product so that you are not falling so deeply in love with it that you don't see the potential flaws. While passion is important, you also need to have an open mind and listen to your customers. Your customers will tell you the truth because they made the purchase.
- Cultivate an environment where passion is not only acknowledged but actively encouraged. It becomes the driving force that infuses creativity into problem-solving and resilience in the face of challenges.

Faith: An Anchor in the Entrepreneurial Voyage:

- Cultivate unwavering faith in your vision, even in uncertainties. Your unwavering belief becomes the anchor that steadies the ship during stormy seas.
- Share your faith with your team and stakeholders. It serves as a guiding light, fostering a collective sense of purpose and determination.

Belief in Your Product: The Catalyst for Conviction:

- Nurture a deep and unshakeable belief in the value your product brings to the market. This conviction is contagious; it resonates with potential customers, investors, and collaborators.
- Continuously reinforce your belief by staying attuned to customer testimonials, positive feedback, and the real-world impact your product has. This steadfast belief becomes a powerful catalyst for success.

Transparency and Authenticity: Strengthening Connections:

- Transparency and Authenticity: Strengthening Connections: Infuse transparency and authenticity into your communication. Share not only the triumphs but also the challenges and lessons learned.
- Authenticity builds trust, strengthening the connection between you and your audience. Transparent communication enhances the credibility of your passion and beliefs.

Maintaining Enthusiasm in Adversity: Resilience as a Testament:

- Embrace challenges as opportunities for growth. Let your passion and belief serve as a wellspring of resilience.
- Cultivate an attitude that sees setbacks as temporary and navigable. This resilient mindset, fueled by passion, helps you persevere when faced with adversity.

Inspiring Your Team: Shared Vision for Collective Triumph:
- Inspire and motivate your team by transmitting your passion and belief in the product.
- Encourage a shared vision, fostering a collective sense of purpose. An inspired team becomes a dynamic force capable of overcoming challenges and contributing innovative ideas.

Connecting with Your Audience: Emotional Bonds Through Storytelling:
- Share your journey authentically through compelling storytelling. Convey the passion, challenges, and triumphs that define your venture.
- Emotional connections are forged when your audience can relate to the human aspects of your entrepreneurial journey

Adapting Passion to Market Dynamics: Flexibility in Conviction:
- While unwavering in your belief, remain adaptable to changing market dynamics.
- Recognize the need for adjustments based on feedback, emerging trends, and shifting consumer preferences. Passion, when coupled with adaptability, ensures your product remains relevant and resilient.

Celebrating Milestones: Nourishing the Spirit of Triumph:
- Acknowledge and celebrate every milestone achieved on your journey.
- Celebrations serve as reminders of progress, boost team morale, and reinforce your faith in the venture. Milestones, big or small, are significant steps toward the realization of your passion-fueled vision.

Sharing Success Stories: Amplifying Impact and Inspiration:
- Share success stories that highlight the positive impact your product has on customers' lives.
- These stories are potent testimonials, inspiring your team and serving as effective marketing tools. Their real-world impact underscores the importance of your passion and belief.

As you immerse yourself in the heart and soul of your entrepreneurial venture, recognize that passion, faith, and belief are dynamic forces intricately shaping the narrative of your journey. These elements extend beyond personal sentiments, resonating profoundly not only within yourself but also with those who become part of your entrepreneurial odyssey.

In the complex pathways of entrepreneurship, kindness emerges as an essential companion to your passion and faith. It is the gentle touch that infuses empathy into your interactions—both with yourself and others. Cultivating a supportive team environment involves acknowledging individual efforts, fostering a collaborative spirit, and expressing gratitude. This kindness becomes a driving force, propelling your venture forward.

Amidst the inevitable challenges, fortifying your positivity is crucial. Kindness acts as a shield, preventing negativity from overshadowing the optimism that fuels your journey. It includes practicing self-compassion, viewing setbacks as opportunities for growth, and promoting a culture of constructive feedback within your team. Remember, as you navigate the exciting and challenging terrain of entrepreneurship, kindness becomes the compass guiding decisions and shaping the character of your venture. Success is not solely about reaching the destination; it's about the positive and lasting impact created along the way. So, nurture the seeds of kindness in your entrepreneurial journey and witness them blossom into a garden of success, empathy, and fulfillment.

Step *into*

your journey *with*

blinders *on both sides*

and don't be

distracted

by the noise

Lisa Marie Ascolese

CHRONICLES OF TRIUMPH - THE SIGNIFICANCE OF JOURNALING YOUR ENTREPRENEURIAL JOURNEY

Embarking on the penultimate chapter of your entrepreneurial saga, we explore a practice that transcends the written word—it's the art of journaling. Chapter Ten delves into the profound importance of documenting your journey, both for personal reflection and as a strategic tool for navigating the challenges and triumphs of entrepreneurship. This chapter not only underscores the benefits of journaling but also introduces seven dedicated pages for you to record your thoughts, insights, and milestones.

The Power of Reflection: Crafting a Personal Narrative:
- Journaling provides a space for introspection, allowing you to reflect on your experiences, decisions, and emotions.
- Create a personal narrative that captures the essence of your entrepreneurial journey. As you revisit your entries, patterns and insights will emerge, aiding in personal growth and strategic refinement.

Learning from Challenges: Turning Obstacles into Wisdom:
- Documenting challenges encountered along the way transforms them into valuable lessons.

- Explore the root causes, your responses, and the outcomes. Journaling serves as a repository of wisdom, helping you navigate similar obstacles in the future with greater insight and resilience.

Celebrating Triumphs: Anchoring Moments of Success:
- Record moments of triumph, big and small. These victories become anchors that fortify your resolve during challenging times.
- Revisit these entries to relish the sense of accomplishment, reinforcing your confidence and motivation to overcome future hurdles. It's important to look back so you can see how far you have come. When we are moving forward and constantly trying to build our products and business, at times it can feel like we are pedaling fast and not going anywhere.

Strategic Decision-Making: A Blueprint for Success:
- Use your journal as a tool for strategic decision-making.
- Document the rationale behind pivotal choices, the data considered, and the anticipated outcomes. Over time, this log becomes a strategic blueprint, offering insights into the evolution of your decision-making process.

Evolving Goals and Vision: Dynamic Visionary Record:
- As your venture evolves, so do your goals and vision. Journaling captures the evolution of your aspirations.
- Regularly revisit and update your goals. This practice ensures that your journey aligns with your broader vision and allows for adjustments based on changing circumstances.

Mental and Emotional Well-being: A Therapeutic Outlet:

- Expressing your thoughts and emotions in a journal can be a therapeutic outlet for the stresses of entrepreneurship.
- Use your journal to process challenges, articulate aspirations, and acknowledge personal growth. This practice contributes to your mental and emotional well-being throughout your entrepreneurial voyage.

Track Progress and Milestones: A Motivational Timeline:

- Create a timeline of milestones and progress achieved. Documenting these markers serves as a motivational tool.
- Visually witnessing your journey unfold on paper reinforces the tangible impact of your efforts, fostering a sense of pride and momentum.

Building a Legacy: A Document for Posterity:

- Your journal becomes a living document—a testament to your entrepreneurial legacy.
- Consider it a gift for future generations, showcasing not just the achievements but also the resilience, innovation, and character that defined your journey.

Clarifying Vision and Purpose: A North Star in Uncertainty:

- In moments of uncertainty, revisit your journal to clarify your vision and purpose.
- Your entries serve as a North Star, guiding you back to the core motivations and aspirations that set you on this transformative entrepreneurial path.

Continuous Adaptation: A Living Manuscript of Evolution:

- Your journal is not static; it's a living manuscript that evolves alongside your journey.
- Embrace the continuous adaptation of your journal, mirroring the dynamic nature of entrepreneurship. Allow it to be a canvas for growth, evolution, and the unfolding chapters of your story.

Journaling Pages (Pages 1-7):

- **Page 1:** Reflect on a recent challenge you faced and the lessons learned.

- **Page 2:** Celebrate a recent triumph, big or small, and capture theemotions associated with it and date it.

- **Page 3:** Record a strategic decision you made recently, outlining the factors considered and expected outcomes.

- **Page 4:** Update your current goals and vision. How have they evolved since the start of your journey?

- **Page 5:** Express your current thoughts and emotions related to your entrepreneurial venture.

- **Page 6:** Track recent progress and milestones achieved, noting the impact on your journey.

- **Page 7:** Write a letter to your future self, outlining your aspirations and reflections on your journey so far.

As you embrace the practice of journaling, remember that this isn't just a record—it's a dynamic tool that enhances your resilience, fosters growth, and contributes to the enduring legacy of your entrepreneurial journal.

Explore the art of continual innovation and sustaining momentum. Your story unfolds on these pages; let the ink be a testament to your triumphs.

Walk *in* faith

and truth

and the

rest *is* tiramisu

Lisa Marie Ascolese

ELEVEN

FROM THE BOSOM BUDDY BREAST FEEDING CAPE TO QVC TELEVISION

Since I was nine years old, or as long as I can remember, I have been inventing products. Just taking day-to-day items around the house, redesigning them, and creating something new and more functional for myself was what I did all the time. Being raised in Brooklyn as a child, we played outside all the time.

For some reason, it always felt like summer. I'm saying this to say, that I spent a lot of time on the handball courts in Brooklyn, and if anyone plays handball reading this, you know it's a fast-moving sport, and you need to be quick on your feet, so comfortable sneakers with tight laces are imperative when playing handball. So, what I did was create shoe laces that stayed tied no matter what. That was one of the dozens of products I made as a child. I honestly didn't even think of the items I was making as inventions; I was merely creating products that would make my life more comfortable and easy because I was a very busy child! :) Some things never change.

During that time, I was creating neckwear that is very popular today. I would take old skeleton keys and make necklaces, hair ties, shoe bells for friends, and the list goes on. I'll never forget the first time I embarked on inventing and manufacturing my initial product, many years ago, the "Bosom Buddy Breastfeeding Cape".

My Mommy ❤️

Back then, I didn't quite know what I was doing, but I put my trust and faith in God to guide me, and He did just that. I realized I needed a prototype to bring my vision to life, so I drew up a pattern and cut it out from a sheet of fabric. Then, I approached a local dry cleaner to see if they could help create a few samples.

Armed with fabric I had purchased from a nearby store, I was hopeful. The samples turned out great! Excited but cautious, I tested them out at home without disclosing my project to anyone outside my immediate family. You see, I have this rule: I don't share my ideas until the ink dries—meaning, I wait until they're fully developed. I'm always cautious  about someone unintentionally copying my ideas as you should as I mentioned throughout the book. Non-disclosure agreements and patent protection are imperative! It's not that I don't value advice; I just prefer to share it with trusted individuals who genuinely have my best interests at heart.

The Bosom Buddy was born out of a personal need. As a breastfeeding mother, I found it uncomfortable to nurse in front of others, which I felt would affect my baby's feeding experience.

So, I started brainstorming ways to cover up discreetly while still ensuring my baby was comfortable. And thus, the Bosom Buddy came to be. I ended up selling countless pieces, mostly through word of mouth and by mailing samples to companies.

It turned out to be a successful venture and provided a steady income for a while. Unfortunately, when domestic factories started closing down, I couldn't tap into overseas markets to sustain production, so I had to bid farewell to Bosom Buddy—for the time being.

Now, I'm in the process of redesigning it and working on package designs, which takes time. Over the years, I've learned not to rush a good idea; I let it evolve naturally and stick to my vision.

Slow, focused progress usually pays off in the end. I do my best to explain how important it is to have patience and stay focused on the long-term goal and success of the product, and to not accept the first sample they receive as the production sample but to evaluate it properly and make sure it is correct. This philosophy of being patient is not always an easy process for inventors to practice due to the excitement of just wanting their product finished and on the market, in addition to spending money not knowing whether or not the product is going to sell. It's a very common thing among most inventors; you are not alone in this mindset.

This brings us to another one of my creations—the BunTie hair accessory. It all started by accident. Every Sunday going to church, I'd put my hair up in a bun using a sock. I kept receiving compliments on my hair, and after about the twentieth compliment, I thought,

This could be a product! So, after church one day, I began designing these hair accessories. Initially named "Twist It." It eventually evolved into the BunTie.

I reached out to my friend Cindy Russo, whom I had met during a photo shoot with my daughter Giana, and her son, Johnny, when they were toddlers. Cindy, a QVC product presenter, loved the idea and connected me with a company that manufactured products overseas. Months later, the BunTie prototypes arrived at my doorstep, and it felt like a scene out of a movie all happening in slow motion.

The journey didn't end there. We spent countless hours perfecting the packaging and eventually pitched it to QVC—and they said yes, and one of my biggest highlights was that my daughter Brittany was one of the models showcasing it on air.

I know I just made this sound simple; believe me, it's not!!!! There were many big NO's before there was a yes; there were questions about everything from price points to colors and quantities and back and forth before we got that final yes. I really felt the need to clarify that point because, unless you have tried to market a product, all you see is the end result on a show like QVC or on a store shelf. I can promise you, it took a lot of time, effort, and money to get them through those doors.

Since then, I've had the opportunity to manufacture and showcase hundreds of products on QVC, HSN, and in retail, many of my own and for my clients. I will always be grateful to Cindy for her kindness and for opening a door for me to walk through. Many of my own products as I mentioned earlier, as well as launching products for my clients, it's been quite a blessing throughout my journey.

I'm grateful for the opportunity to have been pursuing my passion for more than thirty-five years. My life's goal has always been to make a difference in the world and to help others, and by God's grace, I'm doing just that. As a girl born in London and raised in Brooklyn, I've come a long way. If I can do it, so can you. Hold onto your dreams, have faith, persevere, and most importantly, believe in yourself.

I hope you enjoyed "The Inventor's Guide to Inventing All or Nothing, Now or Never." If you need any help along your journey, count on me. I have your back! Congratulations in advance on the successful inventing journey you're on!

Never Share

Your Ideas

Until

The Ink

Dries

Lisa Marie Ascolese

Lifting *Each Other* Up

Two Hands

At A Time,

and sometimes

you need a foot

Lisa Marie Ascolese

When you rise

to the top

extend your hand down

and lift

others higher

Lisa Marie Ascolese

Write *Your Dreams*

On Your *White Canvas*

And *Live* Them,

They Belong

To You

Just Ask!

Lisa Marie Ascolese

_____

_____

_____

_____

_____

_____

_____

_____

_____

_____

_____

_____

_____

_____

_____

_____

_____

_____

Journal
Your Journey

_____

_____

_____

_____

_____

_____

_____

_____

_____

_____

_____

_____

_____

_____

_____

Journal
Your Journey

_____

_____

_____

_____

_____

_____

_____

_____

_____

_____

_____

_____

_____

_____

_____

_____

_____

Journal
Your Journey

_____

_____

_____

_____

_____

_____

_____

_____

_____

_____

_____

_____

_____

_____

_____

_____

Journal
Your Journey

_____

_____

_____

_____

_____

_____

_____

_____

_____

_____

_____

_____

_____

_____

_____

_____

Journal
Your Journey

_____

_____

_____

_____

_____

_____

_____

_____

_____

_____

_____

_____

_____

_____

_____

_____

Journal
Your Journey

_____

_____

_____

_____

_____

_____

_____

_____

_____

_____

_____

_____

_____

_____

_____

_____

_____

_____

Journal
Your Journey

_____

_____

_____

_____

_____

_____

_____

_____

_____

_____

_____

_____

_____

_____

_____

_____

Journal
Your Journey

_____

_____

_____

_____

_____

_____

_____

_____

_____

_____

_____

_____

_____

_____

_____

_____

_____

Journal
Your Journey

_____

_____

_____

_____

_____

_____

_____

_____

_____

_____

_____

_____

_____

_____

_____

_____

_____

Journal
Your Journey

I'm so

proud

of you! ♥

Lisa Marie Ascolese